Maximizing
Your
Impact for
God

INFLUENCE

Interactions Small Group Series

Authenticity: Being Honest with God and Others
Big Questions: Clear Answers to Confusing Issues
Celebrating God: Discover the Truth of God's Character
Character: Reclaiming Six Endangered Qualities
Commitment: Developing Deeper Devotion to Christ
Community: Building Relationships within God's Family
Essential Christianity: Practical Steps for Spiritual Growth
Excellent Living: Giving God Your Best
Fruit of the Spirit: Living the Supernatural Life
Getting a Grip: Finding Balance in Your Daily Life
Influence: Maximizing Your Impact for God
Jesus: Seeing Him More Clearly
Lessons on Love: Building Deeper Relationships
Living in God's Power: Finding God's Strength for Life's Challenges
Love in Action: Experiencing the Joy of Serving
Marriage: Building Real Intimacy
Meeting God: Psalms for the Highs and Lows of Life
New Identity: Discovering Who You Are in Christ
Parenting: How to Raise Spiritually Healthy Kids
Prayer: Opening Your Heart to God
Reaching Out: Sharing God's Love Naturally
The Real Deal: Discover the Rewards of Authentic Relationships
Significance: Understanding God's Purpose for Your Life
Transformation: Letting God Change You from the Inside Out

Maximizing
Your
Impact for
God

INFLUENCE

BILL HYBELS
WITH KEVIN AND SHERRY HARNEY

ZONDERVAN.com/
AUTHORTRACKER
follow your favorite authors

ZONDERVAN

Influence

Requests for information should be addressed to:

Zondervan, *Grand Rapids, Michigan 49530*

ISBN 978-0-310-28066-8

Cover and interior design by Rick Devon and Michelle Espinoza

Printed in the United States of America

09 10 11 12 13 14 15 16 17 18 • 20 19 18 17 16 15 14 13 12 11 10 9 8 7 6 5 4 3 2 1

Contents

Interactions

In 1992, Willow Creek Community Church, in partnership with Zondervan and the Willow Creek Association, released a curriculum for small groups entitled the Walking with God series. In just three years, almost a half million copies of these small group study guides were being used in churches around the world. The phenomenal response to this curriculum affirmed the need for relevant and biblical small group materials.

At the writing of this curriculum, there were nearly 3,000 small groups meeting regularly within the structure of Willow Creek Community Church. We believe this number will increase as we continue to place a central value on small groups. Many other churches throughout the world are growing in their commitment to small group ministries as well, so the need for resources is increasing.

In response to this great need, the Interactions small group series has been developed. Willow Creek Association and Zondervan have joined together to create a whole new approach to small group materials. These discussion guides are meant to challenge group members to a deeper level of sharing, create lines of accountability, move followers of Christ into action, and help group members become fully devoted followers of Christ.

Suggestions for Individual Study

1. Begin each session with prayer. Ask God to help you understand the passage and to apply it to your life.
2. A good modern translation, such as the New International Version, Today's New International Version, the New American Standard Bible, or the New Revised Standard Version, will give you the most help. Questions in this guide are based on the New International Version.
3. Read and reread the passage(s). You must know what the passage says before you can understand what it means and how it applies to you.
4. Write your answers in the spaces provided in the study guide. This will help you to express clearly your understanding of the passage.
5. Keep a Bible dictionary handy. Use it to look up unfamiliar words, names, or places.

Suggestions for Group Study

1. Come to the session prepared. Careful preparation will greatly enrich your time in group discussion.
2. Be willing to join in the discussion. The leader of the group will not be lecturing but will encourage people to discuss what they have learned in the passage. Plan to share what God has taught you in your individual study.
3. Stick to the passage being studied. Base your answers on the verses being discussed rather than on outside authorities such as commentaries or your favorite author or speaker.
4. Try to be sensitive to the other members of the group. Listen attentively when they speak, and be affirming whenever you can. This will encourage more hesitant members of the group to participate.
5. Be careful not to dominate the discussion. By all means participate, but allow others to have equal time.
6. If you are the discussion leader, you will find additional suggestions and helpful ideas in the Leader's Notes.

Additional Resources and Teaching Materials

At the end of this study guide you will find a collection of resources and teaching materials to help you in your growth as a follower of Christ. You will also find resources that will help your church develop and build fully devoted followers of Christ.

Introduction: Maximizing Your Impact for God

You are a person of influence. If you can take a breath, feel your pulse, and interact with other human beings, you are making a difference. Your life has a bigger impact on other people than you know or dream. You have influence!

This is very easy to forget. In a time when celebrities, rock stars, politicians, and business titans receive saturation-level media coverage, we mistakenly assume that our own influence is inconsequential. On the contrary, God has made you to have significant impact on the people around you.

Parents have great influence in the lives of their children. Grandparents can make a huge difference in grandchildren's lives. Teachers have far more impact on the shaping of lives than they can fully comprehend. Leaders in the workplace have an effect every single day on those they supervise and interact with. Sunday school teachers, small group leaders, youth workers, church board members, and so many others who volunteer in the church are touching countless lives. The list could go on and on. Every one of us has potential to influence people every day. Our attitudes, behaviors, choices, words, and even facial expressions make a difference.

One day the most influential person who ever walked this planet gave His views on this very topic. If I could distill His teachings into a three-word sound bite, it would be: MAXIMIZE YOUR INFLUENCE. One day Jesus was speaking to His followers, people who were in various stages of spiritual development, and He used the metaphor of light and darkness to make His point. Jesus said:

"You are the light of the world. A city on a hill cannot be hidden. Neither do people light a lamp and put it under a bowl. Instead they put it on its stand, and it gives light to everyone in the house. In the same way, let your light shine before men, that they may see your good deeds and praise your Father in heaven." (Matthew 5:14–16)

Picture a small house lit by a single oil lamp. The light shines and fills the living area and illuminates the whole house. Then someone decides to minimize the light by grabbing a bowl and putting it over the lamp. Very quickly the house grows dark. Another person decides it makes more sense to put the lamp on a stand where it can lend even more illuminating power to the room and the house. Jesus is saying, that's the right idea! Let's think in terms of bringing more light, more influence, to the world. Put the lamp up on a stand.

Take note that the brightness of the oil lamp does not change at all during Jesus' illustration. The lamp just shines the way lamps do. What actually changes is the location of the lamp. The light-giving potential varies depending on where the oil lamp is placed . . . on a stand or under a bowl.

The implications of this teaching are absolutely profound. Jesus was helping His followers see that darkness was encroaching. He wanted them to look around their world just like He wants us to take note of what is happening around us today. We don't have to look far to see oppression, injustice, greed, violence, and sin of all kinds. Evil is on the loose with menacing tenacity. Darkness is descending on the land.

Jesus speaks today with the same urgency He spoke two thousand years ago: "You are like oil lamps. You have enough candlepower to give light to the people I want you to influence. The real question is not, 'Does your life shine?' but, 'Will you make decisions that will put your light on a stand rather than under a bowl.' " The decision is really up to us.

Jesus is calling us to worry a little *less* about our candlepower and to focus more on leveraging the light we have so that everyone in our arena of influence can receive God's light shining through us.

That is the focus of this six-week study: Letting the light of God's presence and truth shine freely through us. It is about positioning our life on a stand so that we can have maximum influence and impact. This influence spans a broad spectrum ranging from meeting daily needs all the way to presenting the message of salvation found in Jesus Christ. As we follow Him, God will bring maximum influence that will reveal His presence, bring His gospel, and change the world for His glory.

DAILY INFLUENCE

THE BIG PICTURE

On a flight from the West Coast back to Chicago, I had a perspective-giving encounter. After learning that the gentleman seated next to me was from the Chicago area, I asked him, "Where are you from in Chicago?" He answered, "Well, I'm actually from a little town called South Barrington."

I said, "No kidding. What do you do there?"

He replied, "I'm a doctor in South Barrington . . . have been for twenty years."

He then asked me, "Where are you from?"

I said, "Well, interestingly, I live and work in Barrington too."

He immediately asked me, "What do you do?"

I said, "I've been the pastor of Willow Creek Community Church for a long, long time."

He said, "Really . . . never heard of it. Is it Catholic or Protestant?"

In that moment I felt a twinge of that ever-present enticement to think, "Maybe my life is not as significant as I hoped it would be."

I am convinced that most of us fall into this dangerous line of thinking. And when such a mind-set wins out, we would never dare lie awake at night dreaming about how to maximize our influence. Instead, we begin to entertain thoughts like: "I don't have much to offer. If I were in the public eye, if others recognized me, or if the media sought me out, I might worry about how to leverage my life. But I'm just me in my little world. So I'll put a bowl over my head and not think much about letting my light shine."

A WIDE ANGLE VIEW

1

Tell about a time something happened that made you wonder if you could really have a significant impact on the lives of others.

When situations, voices, or something in your heart make you think you will never be a person of influence, how do you battle against these lies?

A BIBLICAL PORTRAIT

Read 1 Corinthians 13

2

This classic Bible passage features a list of things that love *is* and things that love *is not*. Each time we read what love is, we can turn the statement around and discover what love is not. In the same way, when we read what love is not, we can reverse the concept and discover what it is. As a group, use the passage to complete the table below. Be sure to give an illustration for each set of opposites.

Love Is ...	Love Is Not ...	Illustration

3 In the beginning of this passage the apostle Paul is clear that the use of spiritual gifts, the display of great knowledge or faith, and powerful acts of generosity must be done in love if they are going to have maximum impact. How does love act as a governing force as we seek to impact our world and influence the people around us?

SHARPENING THE FOCUS

Read Snapshot "Spread Love"

SPREAD LOVE

Have you ever heard of Maslow's Hierarchy of Needs? It is a school of thinking (put in a very basic way) that espouses the idea that our developmental needs begin with the basics. Once our basic needs are met, we are free to go about meeting a higher set of needs. Eventually, as we get these higher needs met, we reach a point of self-actualization. When we think about how God wants us to exercise influence, this basic idea comes to mind. We should try to have influence and meet needs on basic levels first and then direct our energy to having influence in more complex areas of life and culture.

If I were to identify one of the most basic and foundational ways we can have daily influence, I would begin with the commitment to *spread love.* In 1 Corinthians 13 we discover that three things will always remain . . . faith, hope, and love. But the apostle Paul is quick to declare, "The greatest of these is love" (v. 13). All of us would have a greater and more positive influence if we were known as people of love. One of the most natural and powerful ways we can touch the lives of those around us is to let love flow freely from us to them.

4 Tell about a person in your life who has consistently and freely shown love to you.

How has their life influenced yours?

5 What specific act of love could you extend to someone in the coming week that would have a positive, Christ-honoring impact?

How can your group members pray for you and keep you accountable as you spread love in this way?

Read Snapshot "Meet Needs"

MEET NEEDS

Once we are seeking to spread love and to have influence by meeting this need in people's lives, we can take the next step. Along with expressing God's love, we can take steps to meet daily and practical needs. In Acts 2:42–47 we discover that the early church became known for the ways they met the needs of others.

Willow Creek Community Church has a sister church located in a tiny village of about a thousand people just outside the capital of Costa Rica in Central America. When that church was very small, the pastor and a core of leaders decided they were going to try to influence their community by meeting basic needs. They would consistently and joyfully assist the poor, care for wayward kids, serve people with addictions, and get elbow-deep in all the messy problems that exist in their community. Ten years later, about seven hundred of the thousand people in that town are a part of that one church. What a testimony to the power of influence that comes when we meet needs in the name and grace of Jesus.

6 Picture a local church and individual believers who consistently seek to meet the needs present in their neighborhood and surrounding community. How can such acts of service open the door for influence?

Picture a local congregation and the Christians in a community who never act to meet needs and help the people in their neighborhood. What messages does this send to the people of the community?

7

As you look at where God has placed your church or the neighborhood where you live, talk about some of the needs that could be met there.

What is one step you could take to be part of God's plan to care for people in your community?

Read Snapshot "Confront Injustice"

CONFRONT INJUSTICE

When we are engaged in spreading love and meeting needs, we can then dial things up another notch. In the name of Jesus and by His power, we can begin to confront injustice . . . in our personal lives, as small groups, and as a church. This can take countless shapes and forms.

God's people can feed the hungry, speak up for those who do not have a voice, seek racial reconciliation with people groups who feel ostracized and marginalized, protect the lives of unborn children, provide clothing for those who are under-resourced, and the list goes on and on. Wherever there is injustice, God's people can exercise influence by confronting it.

8

Cite some examples you have seen or heard of where Christians (or groups of believers) are confronting injustice and making a difference in the name of Jesus.

9

What are some of the injustices that exist in your community?

What could your church or small group do to exercise influence and confront one or more of these injustices?

PUTTING YOURSELF IN THE PICTURE

A Big Thank-You!

We all know people who have used their influence to impact our life and the lives of others. These influencers often make a big difference, yet we sometimes forget to thank or encourage them for what they've done. Identify one such person and take time to let them know how they have touched your life. Write a note, send an email, make a phone call, or plan for a personal visit. Let them know the difference God has made in your life through them.

Growing in Love

Print out the text of 1 Corinthians 13:4–7 and highlight all of the things that love is and is not. Then keep this paper in your purse or wallet so that you can easily meditate on it once or twice a week. Each time you read the passage, pray for power to spread God's love in natural and life-influencing ways.

DEEPER INFLUENCE

REFLECTIONS FROM SESSION 1

1. Tell about a recent step you have taken to intentionally extend love to someone in your circle of influence.
2. How have you been seeking to meet needs in new and fresh ways since the last time your group met?
3. If you have been noticing some of the injustice in the world, what have you seen and how has God been stirring your heart to confront it?

THE BIG PICTURE

In a world of darkness, God wants His light to shine. For some amazing reason, one of the primary ways He does this is through ordinary people. Every man, woman, and child who follows Jesus has the potential to reflect the light of God into dark situations and thereby bring heavenly influence. This influence comes in ordinary and daily ways as we spread love, meet needs, and confront injustice.

Sometimes our opportunities for influence go deeper still as our eyes are opened to see things we would rather not think about or deal with. In this place of spiritual awareness our hearts are typically broken over all the pain and violence in the world.

One year at the Willow Creek Leadership Summit, Gary Haugen, a Harvard-trained Christian attorney and author of the book *Just Courage*, spoke about this deeper level of influence. He brought a message that affirmed the call to spread love, meet needs, and confront injustice; then he challenged attendees to go a step further by helping to put an end to the horrible acts of violence and abuse that take place all over the world on a daily basis.

It will take a deep commitment and powerful influence to put an end to things like child prostitution, sex trafficking, slave labor, political beatings, false incarcerations, and marginalization of entire people groups. Or to help change the violent systems that keep people in poverty. Indeed, when we commit to make a difference on this deep of a level, it will take the power of God's Spirit working through us .... and He will do so in ways that will amaze and surprise us.

A WIDE ANGLE VIEW

1 Some believers look at the magnitude of the world's problems and feel overwhelmed and under equipped to deal with them. They might declare, "I'm just one person . . . I can't make a difference." What might Jesus say to such Christians?

A BIBLICAL PORTRAIT

Read Psalm 140

2 In this short psalm, David addresses the reality of violence in the world. What does this psalm teach about those who are violent and who create oppressive systems of violence?

3 How might David's prayer (specifically vv. 8–10) shape the way you pray against cruel and violent people?

What does this psalm teach about how God feels about violence and His response to those who abuse and attack innocent people?

SHARPENING THE FOCUS

Read Snapshot "Stemming the Tide of Violence"

STEMMING THE TIDE OF VIOLENCE

Those who stand against violence often find themselves in the middle of a firestorm. Let's not kid ourselves, seeking to exercise influence on this level can be dangerous and costly. When Nelson Mandela stood against apartheid, he was abused, slandered, and imprisoned. His resistance to this evil system brought violence to him and those he loved. When Dr. Martin Luther King Jr. resisted the violence and injustice of racism in the United States, he became a victim of the very evil he was battling. Those who seek to save children and women from slavery and prostitution will incur the wrath of those who make money from these violent and oppressive systems.

If we are going to exercise influence against the violent, brutal systems of this world, we must realize that we are walking onto a battlefield. Victory will come only with the strength of God filling us, and with brothers and sisters standing at our side.

4 Sometimes it is easier to look the other way, to ignore the violence that exists in our communities and world. What are some of the coping mechanisms we can put in place to build a buffer between us and the violence around us?

God wants us to see what He sees and feel what He feels so that we will be moved to action. What can we do to open our eyes and hearts to victims of violence?

5 What are some of the violent systems that exist in:

- Your neighborhood or local community?
- Your nation?
- The world?

What practical steps and actions can a follower of Christ take to resist and battle against one of these violent systems?

Read Snapshot "Reconciling People to God"

RECONCILING PEOPLE TO GOD

Followers of Christ can use their influence to spread love, meet needs, confront injustice, and overcome violence. All of these are important and should be a regular part of the landscape of our life. But there is one more area that must always be a high priority as we let God's light shine and influence others. God wants to use you and me in His work of reconciling people to Himself.

A number of times in Jesus' ministry people pressed Him to name His main purpose, His highest priority. To which Jesus replied, "[I] came to seek and to save what was lost" (Luke 19:10). Jesus came to remove the barriers that keep people from a relationship with God. He came to be the bridge between people far from the Father, to reconcile them. And He was clear that this should be at the top of our priority list as well.

6 After Jesus died on the cross to pay the price for human sins and rose again in victory over the grave and death, He gave His followers clear instructions before He ascended to heaven:

Then Jesus came to them and said, "All authority in heaven and on earth has been given to me. Therefore go and make disciples of all nations, baptizing them in the name of the Father and of the Son and of the Holy Spirit, and teaching them to obey everything I have commanded you. And surely I am with you always, to the very end of the age." (Matthew 28:18–20)

"But you will receive power when the Holy Spirit comes on you; and you will be my witnesses in Jerusalem, and in all Judea and Samaria, and to the ends of the earth." (Acts 1:8)

As you look at Christians today, how are we doing in this mission of being witnesses and making disciples?

As you look at the local church, how are congregations doing at fulfilling this Great Commission?

7 Some followers of Jesus shine God's light by spreading love and meeting needs but are reluctant to speak the message of the cross and call people to repent from sin and follow Jesus. Others are quick to bring the message of Jesus and call people to receive Him, but they neglect to meet needs and spread love in their actions. What are the potential dangers of each of these extremes?

Read Snapshot "Striking a God-Honoring Balance"

STRIKING A GOD-HONORING BALANCE

The early church was vigorous, rigorous, and fearless with its proclamation of the message of reconciliation to God through faith in Jesus. It sought to spread God's love through meeting human needs and confronting injustice with unwavering passion. In no sense was the call to serve humbly and battle injustice disconnected from the proclamation of salvation found in Jesus Christ.

Over the past century, the Western church has become unbalanced in its focus — proclaiming the message of reconciliation to the neglect of meeting needs or overcoming injustice or getting elbow-deep in people's messy problems.

In response, others in the Western church have let the pendulum swing to the opposite extreme — the "restoration" aspects of God's work in the world. For them, helping the poor, doing AIDS relief, and providing clean water have become the *whole* message of the gospel. They lovingly meet people's physical needs but forget that without a relationship with the Savior, these very same people are facing a Christless eternity.

8 How would you rate your church on the scale below?

Focused on physical needs — *Balanced* — *Focused on spiritual needs*

1 2 3 4 5 6 7 8 9 10

What is one step your church could take to strike a stronger balance?

9 How would you rate yourself on the scale below?

Focused on physical needs				*Balanced*					*Focused on spiritual needs*
1	*2*	*3*	*4*	*5*	*6*	*7*	*8*	*9*	*10*

What is one step you could take to strike a stronger balance?

PUTTING YOURSELF IN THE PICTURE

Opposing Violence

Take time in the coming week to answer the questions below:

- What is one kind of violent behavior or system that exists within my community?
- How can I pray against this behavior or system?
- How can I be part of God's work in overcoming this violence, letting His light shine through me?
- Who can I partner with in this ministry?

After you have answered the questions, begin to pray and take action. Enter in and expect God to let His light shine in and through you.

I Am God's Reconciler

In the coming weeks we will dig deeper into God's plan to use us in His work of reconciliation. As you prepare for this, meditate on and consider memorizing the following passage:

All this is from God, who reconciled us to himself through Christ and gave us the ministry of reconciliation: that God was reconciling the world to himself in Christ, not counting men's sins against them. And he has committed to us the message of reconciliation. We are therefore Christ's ambassadors, as though God were making his appeal through us. We implore you on Christ's behalf: Be reconciled to God. (2 Corinthians 5:18–20)

Eternal Influence

Reflections from Session 2

1. The last time your group met you began thinking about the reality of violence in the world and the call for Christ-followers to work against it. How have you been sensitized to the presence of violence, and how has God stirred your heart to notice and care?
2. One of the "Putting Yourself in the Picture" challenges invited you to spend time meditating on 2 Corinthians 5:18–20. This passage reminds us that we are reconciled to God and are called to be God's ambassador of reconciliation. If you have been reflecting on this passage, what has God been teaching you?

THE BIG PICTURE

When my son Todd was five years old, he would beg me to take him windsurfing. Because I had spent a lot of time windsurfing on Lake Michigan and was confident he would be safe, once I got going at a pretty good clip I would let him climb up me, swing his legs around my neck, and sit on my shoulders. We would windsurf that way for hours. Todd loved it!

One day, however, as we windsurfed far off the beach, a storm came up suddenly and without warning a wave catapulted me and Todd off the board. My last thought as we were flying through the air was: "I've got to get this kid off my shoulders and free of the rig." Thankfully Todd flew free of the board and sail, but I got caught up in it.

When I finally came to the surface of the water, I couldn't see Todd. Though he could swim a bit, the waves were big and I could not find him. I started screaming for him, calling his name at the top of my lungs, and swimming back and forth in search of my boy.

In that moment I realized how much a missing son meant. Nothing else in the world mattered. As I prayed and searched, my heart ached!

All of a sudden I saw Todd's blond hair on one side of a wave. I kicked and swam like an outboard motor, wrapped my arm around him, and brought him back to the windsurfer. A joy and peace hit me when I found my boy and knew he would be all right.

I pulled his little face close to mine and whispered, "Your mother never needs to know about this."

A WIDE ANGLE VIEW

1 Tell about a time you lost someone or something precious to you, and describe how you felt as you searched for it.

A BIBLICAL PORTRAIT

Read Luke 15

2 What similar themes do you see in the three parables in Luke 15?

3 These three stories teach us a great deal about the heart of God *and* about ourselves. What do you learn about God in these stories?

What do you learn about people?

SHARPENING THE FOCUS

Read Snapshot "Something of Value Is Missing"

SOMETHING OF VALUE IS MISSING

In each of the three stories in Luke 15 something of value winds up missing: a sheep, a coin, a son. One of the reasons Jesus tells the stories just the way He does is that He wants the Pharisees (the religious leaders of the day) to figure out an important truth on their own.

If a shepherd has a hundred sheep and one wanders away, does it really matter? In the culture of that day, shepherds spent so much time with their sheep that they knew each one. They were like pets. If you have a cat or a dog that you love like crazy, you might have a sense of what sheep meant to their shepherd. If your dog wanders off, you would go looking for it. That is the way a shepherd saw a lost sheep.

In the story of the woman and her coin, many Bible scholars think that the coin could have represented a tenth of her estate . . . a big chunk of all she had. It was of great importance to her.

And what of a parent who loses a child? It does not matter if it is in a far-off land or in a stormy lake; a parent who loses a son or daughter knows that something of inexpressible value is missing.

The point of all this is that people matter to God! His heart aches for those who are still wandering and who have not come home. God's disposition toward lost people is not anger and disgust; it is longing and love. Lost people matter to God.

4 What are some other biblical passages, teachings, and confirmations that "people matter to God"?

How should this simple reality impact the way you interact with people as you walk through your day?

Read Snapshot "Worth a Search"

WORTH A SEARCH

A second theme in the three stories of Luke 15 is that a serious, all-out search is warranted because the sheep, coin, and son are so valuable. It's an inconvenience for the shepherd to go into the open country looking for the sheep that wandered away. But the shepherd does it. No one likes to turn a house upside down to find one coin but the woman does it because the coin is so important and needs to be found. Even the father searched the horizon every day, hoping and praying his son would come home.

Jesus tells these three stories exactly the way He does because in an unguarded moment, He wants the Pharisees to think, "Could it be that Jesus was teaching that wayward, wandering people matter, that they are so valuable that God diligently searches for them"? That would be a radical thought for a Pharisee, who thought that God saw sinful people as worthless. In the mind of a Pharisee, people who rebel against God and thumb their nose at Him every day deserve judgment, not a search party that seeks to bring them home.

5 What has God done throughout history (including today) to search, seek, and find His lost sheep?

Tell a little about the search party God sent out to find you.

6 Followers of Jesus are expected to have hearts that beat like His. We are called to be more and more like our Good Shepherd. What are ways that the local church can be more committed to searching for those who are still lost?

How can we individually develop a habit of seeking for lost people as we go about our daily routines and relationships?

Read Snapshot "Party Time"

PARTY TIME

A third common theme that weaves through all three stories in Luke 15 is that each one ends with a party! When the sheep is retrieved, the coin is found, and the son comes home, it is time to celebrate. When the shepherd finds the wayward sheep, he doesn't beat it, but gently scoops it up in his arms, takes it back to the fold, and has a party with his shepherd friends. The woman who finally finds her missing coin calls her friends and neighbors over for a celebration. And the most famous celebration of all comes when the son returns and his dad throws a massive block party. That which was missing mattered so much, and the search was so difficult, that when the retrieval occurred, there was unprecedented joy.

7 What are some visible ways that churches and believers can celebrate (join the heavenly party) when someone comes to faith in Jesus?

Read Snapshot "This Is Urgent"

THIS IS URGENT

If a child is injured, you rush them to the hospital. It is urgent! If you see smoke billowing from a neighbor's house, you don't wait fifteen minutes and then call the fire department, you dial 911 now. It is urgent. When a sheep wanders off, when a valuable coin is lost, when a child wanders away, these are all urgent situations. As God looks at people who are wandering from him like sheep without a shepherd, He sees this as an urgent moment. And He wants us to see it that way too. Lost people matter to God, they are worth a search, and when they finally come home, it is time to party. Now is the time to get involved in the urgent call to help God reconcile people to Himself through His only Son Jesus.

8 What are some ways your church seeks to reach out with the love of God into your community?

How can you engage in these outreach opportunities and support one or more of these efforts?

Name one person wandering far from God about whom you feel urgent.

What could you do in the coming week to connect with this person, pray for this person, or do something that could be part of God's plan to invite them "home"?

PUTTING YOURSELF IN THE PICTURE

Loving Lost Sheep

Read Luke 15 slowly and thoughtfully this week. Then pray about the people you know and care about who are still lost sheep. Make a list of these people and commit to pray for them regularly as you continue this small group study.

Names:

Prayer Focus:

- Pray for the hearts of lost sheep to become tender to the Great Shepherd.
- Pray for ears of lost people to hear the voice of God calling them.
- Ask God to give you a gentle boldness as you seek to let the light of God shine through your life.
- Invite the Holy Spirit to use you, in any way and at any time, to share the love and message of Jesus with people who matter to God but are not yet part of His family.

Time to Connect

God calls those who know Him to let their light shine! This happens best when the lamp is on a stand and not under a bowl. Watch yourself through the coming week and identify ways you can place your light up on a stand. One of the best ways to do this is to spend time with people who are still walking in darkness and living far from God. Make a commitment to spend some time each week with a friend, family member, or neighbor who is not yet a follower of Jesus.

THE ANATOMY OF SPIRITUAL INFLUENCE

REFLECTIONS FROM SESSION 3

1. How have you seen yourself noticing lost people and seeking to enter God's adventure of reaching them with His love and grace?
2. If you have been taking time to pray for people who are far from God, how has this impacted the way you see them and interact with them?
3. Tell about one way you have been seeking to connect in more consistent and meaningful ways with people in your life who are spiritually disconnected.

THE BIG PICTURE

Sitting on a sailboat in a harbor on the Michigan side of Lake Michigan, I got the idea to sail across the lake. So I took out the charts, planned my trip, and headed to the Wisconsin side. When I arrived many hours later, I tidied up the boat, secured it, and began looking at the charts again to decide where I might cruise the next day.

Reviewing the charts, I realized I was within ten miles of the camp where, as a seventeen-year-old, I had received Christ as my Savior. I had a prompting from God, kind of a whisper, nudging me to travel to the camp and stand right on the spot where I became a Christian.

Of course, I had come by water, so transportation was a problem. I called the only cab company in the town, but they couldn't take me because it was just outside their range. When I asked the dispatcher if she knew anybody who might be able to help me, she said she had a friend who was down on his luck and he'd do almost anything for money.

That should have been a clue, right?

I called her friend. I think I woke him out of a dead sleep in the middle of the afternoon. I explained my dilemma and when he heard the word "money," he said he'd be right there. When he pulled into the marina parking lot I could barely believe my eyes. His car was all beat up, a couple of the windows were broken out, and none of the tires was alike. A young man got out and came toward me to shake my hand. He had more tattoos and piercings than I had ever seen on a human body. His hair was scraggly and his jeans were full of holes. But I could sense he was a nice guy.

We climbed into his car and headed toward the camp. We got partway there when I noticed that his car was almost out of gas—the needle was under empty. I'm thinking, "This isn't good." Seeing a gas station ahead, I said, "Hey, if you pull in here, I'll buy you some gas."

He said, "Really?"

I said, "Yeah, because I'd like to get there and back, you know."

He started refueling but only put in about two bucks of gas and then stopped.

I said, "Fill it all the way up."

"Are you paying?"

"Yeah."

He said, "Well, it's never been full before."

I said, "Well, take a risk. Fill it all the way up."

He did. I paid the attendant and we got in the car and headed down the road again. He had a big smile on his face and said, "Handles differently on a full tank of gas."

We finally got out to the camp and I asked him if he would wait for me in the parking lot. I walked to the place where I met Christ. Not everyone can identify the exact place that they first opened their heart to Jesus and prayed, "God, be merciful to me, a sinner," or, "Jesus Christ, I invite you to forgive my sin and lead my life." But for me, I knew the exact spot on that hillside and I went and stood there for the first time in thirty-five years. It was a very powerful, emotional moment for me.

After about twenty minutes a thought flashed through my mind: "I wonder if I lost my ride." I ran back to the parking lot and my driver was still there. "Hey, what were you doing standing out on the side of that hill?" he asked.

"I wanted to come out and stand in the place where I first met God," I replied.

"Really?"

"Yeah."

"Well, how did that happen?"

I asked if he really wanted to know, and he assured me that he did.

I said, "I grew up in a church and it was a good enough church. But it kind of led me to believe that if I was ever going to become a Christian, I would have to strive harder and do a bunch of good deeds; I'd have to clean up my act and fly straight. Then, if I pulled myself together, maybe I'd wind up being a Christian and go to heaven someday. When I went to this camp I heard a verse that said it's not by our own works, but according to God's mercy that He saves us. It's a gift. It's just a gift." (Eph. 2:8)

I told that young man that when I realized that salvation was a gift, that night on a hillside, I received the gift and trusted fully in Christ. I said, "So that's how it happened for me. God met me right there."

The young guy drove for a little while in silence. Then he looked over at me and asked a question I will never forget, "Think God would want to meet a loser like me?"

I said, "Hey, wait. You are not a loser. You were made in the image of God. God loves you, and He's just as ready to meet you and begin a relationship with you as He was ready to meet and begin a relationship with me when I was seventeen years old. You are not a loser. God loves you."

The rest of the way to the marina I explained to him how he could become a Christian. When we arrived he had to get going somewhere so he actually didn't make a commitment to Jesus Christ right then. But he had listened intently. He knew how to become a Christian if he ever wanted to take that step.

A WIDE ANGLE VIEW

1 Tell about a time you were able to talk with someone about the person and message of Jesus. *Or*, tell about a time you were able to tell someone your story of how you became a follower of Jesus.

A BIBLICAL PORTRAIT

Read 2 Corinthians 5:16–21

2 What does the apostle Paul mean by the words "the message of reconciliation"?

What is the role of an ambassador?

3 Once we are reconciled to the Father through faith in Jesus, we are called to be Christ's ambassadors. We are given a ministry of reconciliation. If we are going to live a normal day as an ambassador of Christ, how will this impact:

- Our words?
- Our actions?
- Our attitudes?

- Our interactions?

- Any other part of our day?

SHARPENING THE FOCUS

Read Snapshot "Influential Hands"

INFLUENTIAL HANDS

Let's consider a relationship between two people in which both parties are equally unhappy about the state of it. Their relationship with each other is broken. They're at odds with each other. What was once healthy has gone bad.

Quite often, for two people in this situation to be reconciled, they will need a third party to come alongside them, someone to take the hand of one and gently draw it toward the other. Whether it's a strained marriage, broken friendship, or tense business partnership, this third party might ask, "Are you ready to be reconciled to each other? Is there hope that a healthy and proper relationship could be restored? Could I assist in some way as the two of you seek reconciliation?"

God calls us to do this same thing with people who are far from Him. Every follower of Jesus is invited into a ministry of reconciliation. We have the amazing opportunity to take the hand of a person who is not reconciled to God and put it into the hand of God.

That's all I was trying to do with the young man who drove me to the camp and back. I was trying to take his hand and hook it up with God's hand in some way. I wanted him to know that he could come to know the love of God. He could be reconciled. We can't make people receive Jesus but we can connect a hand to a hand. We can do our part.

4 Tell about one person who helped place your hand in the hand of Jesus. How did they connect you to the Savior? What did they do that felt natural, and what can others learn from their example?

5 Sometimes people shove Jesus in someone's face instead of inviting them to explore Jesus. If you have experienced someone whose tactics were too pushy or forceful, what did you learn from that experience? What outreach approach might you avoid? What

warning would you give to those who tend to push rather than gently invite?

Read Snapshot "Influential Eyes"

INFLUENTIAL EYES

I was driving through downtown Chicago admiring the many landmarks, reflecting on what a fabulous city it is. While looking at new buildings like the Trump Tower and places like Millennium Park, I found myself being thankful that I could live near such an amazing place. All of a sudden I began thinking about a passage in the New Testament:

As [Jesus] approached Jerusalem and saw the city, he wept over it. (Luke 19:41)

Jesus' eyes were not fixed on the physical structures but on the teeming multitudes of people walking around like sheep without a shepherd. My eyes and mind were focused on buildings. I was contrasting different kinds of architecture and noticing only the things that don't last forever. Jesus was looking at people and was profoundly aware that their eternity was hanging in the balance. I was feeling pride for our city . . . Jesus was heartbroken over the condition of people.

It was like a knife in my heart. I prayed, "I need a fresh perspective. God, open my eyes! I want to see people the way Jesus did." Whenever I think back on that experience I am stirred to develop my eyesight so that I see people the way God does.

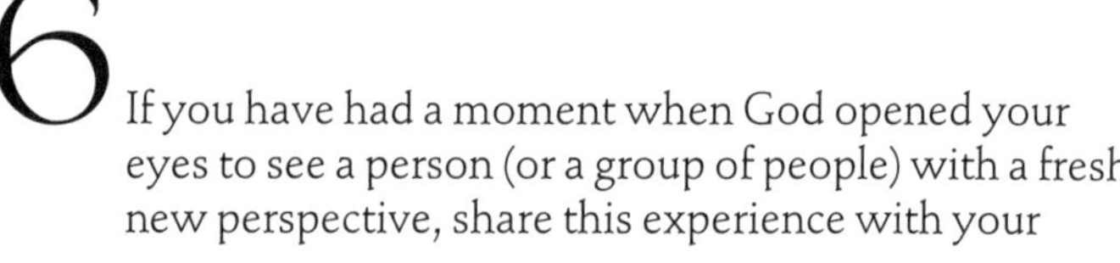

6 If you have had a moment when God opened your eyes to see a person (or a group of people) with a fresh new perspective, share this experience with your group.

7 What are some things (attitudes, actions, motives) that can cloud our vision and keep us from seeing people the way God does?

What can we do to remove obstacles?

Read Snapshot "An Influential Heart"

AN INFLUENTIAL HEART

One of my favorite stories in the Gospels is Matthew's miraculous conversion in Luke 5. For years Matthew had been a tax gatherer. He had cheated people; lived a dishonest and wild life. The people he ran with were not known as the "church-going type."

But when Matthew met Jesus, renounced his sinful past, and began a new life as a Christ follower, an amazing thing happened. Matthew's heart was so touched by Jesus—His love and His grace—that he wanted all his friends to know Him too. So he threw a huge party and invited an A-list of hardcore sinners (fellow tax collectors, prostitutes, etc.) from around town. He also invited his new friends: Jesus and the disciples. What a party! What a picture!

Can you see the love of Matthew? Can you get inside his heart and sense what motivated him? Matthew was longing for Jesus and the disciples to connect with his wild bunch of friends. He had a picture in his mind of what might happen. You can almost hear him wondering, "What if Jesus and the disciples spent some time with these people who are headed in a bad direction? What if Jesus and the disciples befriended my friends, laughed with them, and shared stories about real-life stuff? And what if some of those interactions led to spiritual conversations that would eventually open a door for one of them to be reconciled to God?"

As God moved in Matthew's heart, Matthew got creative and found a way to reach out to those he cared about. In his case, he threw a party. As our heart for people grows, we too will get creative and discover ways to reach out and build bridges. As a group, make a list of various ways we can reach out to those still far from God (these can be individual, small group, or churchwide outreach initiatives).

What is one outreach idea listed above that your small group might use?

PUTTING YOURSELF IN THE PICTURE

Pray for Reconcilers

All of us have people we love and care about who are wandering far from God. In some cases they live a great distance from us and we can't connect with them face-to-face on a regular basis. Be encouraged! God has His reconciling people strategically placed all over the world. Spend time this week praying that God will raise up an ambassador to reach out to your friend or family member you can't spend time with. Ask for the Holy Spirit to give you a calm heart and assurance that God can send someone to bring the message of reconciliation even when you are far away.

Hand in Hand

Each morning I slide out of bed and the first thing that hits the floor are my knees. I kneel there and turn my hands upward on my bed. Then I pray, "God, I'd love to be useful to You today. I would love it if You would work through my life. If there's somebody who's off the path that I could be used to reconcile in some way, and if You want to use me to put someone's hand in Yours, it would be the greatest thing that would happen in my life today. I make myself available." I am convinced that this simple process at the start of each day has opened the way for many wonderful connections with people who need to know the love and grace of God.

For the next week, give this a try. Begin each day on your knees, turn your hands upward, and ask God to use you. Make your hands available. Say, "God, if there is any way you could use me to take the hand of a person and connect it to Your hand, I'm in!"

NATURAL INFLUENCE

REFLECTIONS FROM SESSION 4

1. If you have been praying for eyes like Jesus that see people the way He does, how has this been impacting your daily interactions?
2. If you have had a chance to take the hand of someone and draw it toward the hand of Jesus in some way, share this story.

THE BIG PICTURE

I sat down at a table with eight or nine people I didn't know. The emcee of the event instructed each table's occupants to spend a few minutes getting to know each other. When the African-American gentleman sitting directly opposite me introduced himself, it was clear from his name that he was Muslim. Partway through the meal this man caught my attention and mouthed the words, "I love your books."

I looked over my shoulder to see if an author had come up behind me.

He said, "Let's talk after lunch."

After the lunch he said, "This won't take long, but I owe you a huge debt of gratitude. I'll tell you my story." He told me that when he went off to college the only people who accepted him were Muslims, so he became a Muslim. Eventually he went to grad school and started building his career. His work involved going to a lot of cocktail parties and passing out business cards to generate sales leads. In most cases, he would distribute his cards, then end up standing alone and slipping out as soon as he could.

One night he was standing at a party where five or six guys in a group were having a wonderful conversation. It was pretty obvious it was a closed circle. He'd already passed out his cards and was standing off to the side. This is how my new friend explained what happened next: "One of these white guys from the circle stares across the room and sees me, he really sees me. He extricates himself from this comfortable conversation and walks all the way across the room and sticks out his hand and introduces himself."

The two men had a pleasant conversation. Partway through, the man who walked across the room found out that this African-American was Muslim. Sharing that he was a Christian, he said he didn't know much about Islam and asked if they could go out to breakfast sometime. He said he wasn't planning to change his faith, but he was curious and wanted to learn a little bit about Islam. For the next several weeks they went out to breakfast once a week. After the Muslim guy had given him the scoop on Islam, he told the Christian guy that he'd forgotten most of what he'd learned as a young boy growing up in the church. Maybe the next week the guy could remind him about Christianity and tell him about Jesus again. The Christian guy said, "Okay."

The next several weeks the Christian man told the Muslim man about Jesus, what He did on the cross, the power of the Holy Spirit, and the simple story of faith. After one of these breakfasts the Muslim guy, instead of driving to work, drove home, walked into his bedroom, knelt down by his bed, and asked Christ to come into his life, forgive his sin, and be his leader and guide. Before long, his wife and children received Christ as well.

As he told me his story I was struck by the impact that had been made when one person walked across a room and extended his hand to another.

A WIDE ANGLE VIEW

1 Tell about a time you left a circle or your own comfort zone and reached out to someone who was alone.

What are some reasons this can be such a difficult walk to make?

A BIBLICAL PORTRAIT

Read Acts 16:16–34

2 What consequences did Paul and Silas suffer simply because they sought to speak the truth and share the message of Jesus?

How might this biblical account teach those who feel, "If I just follow God's will, everything will go my way and I will never face hard times"?

3 What surprises or strikes you about Paul and Silas's attitude through this whole experience?

What can we learn from their example and commitment to bring God's message of salvation in Jesus Christ?

SHARPENING THE FOCUS

Read Snapshot "Be an Example of Reconciliation"

BE AN EXAMPLE OF RECONCILIATION

I have three simple coaching tips for those who want to have influence in the lives of others. The first is this: *Live out a fully reconciled life every day.* The vibrancy of our daily life and the authenticity of our faith are more convincing and carry more influence than our best spoken words. If we have been reconciled to the Father through faith in Jesus, and if the Holy Spirit lives in us, God's light will shine through us (Matt. 5:16). Our life is the platform of credibility from which our words will flow.

In the book *Blue Like Jazz*, Donald Miller recounts how he and his Christian friends felt convicted that they had not lived out their Christian faith very well on their secular college campus. One day, after getting kind of a crazy idea from God, they built a shed in the middle of campus and painted the words "Confession Booth" on the front.

When curious students came by and asked about it, Donald and the other Christian students invited them into the shed. Here was the twist. The guests who came into the shed were not asked to confess *their* sins. Instead, they were invited to listen to the Christians confess with honest brokenness how they had failed to live out their faith on that campus — how they had not loved in a way that reflected the depth of God's love, had not helped troubled students enough, had not given enough money for the poor, had not confronted racism with the passion of Jesus. In short, these students reflected an awareness of God's reconciling power in their lives and confessed that they were still learning to be the people He wanted them to be.

4 What are some of the "light-shining" behaviors, practices, and attitudes that will show the world that we have truly been reconciled to God?

5 What are some of the "light-dimming" behaviors, practices, and attitudes that might cause the world to wonder if we are truly in an authentic relationship with God?

How can we battle against these attitudes and actions when they creep into our lives and churches?

Read Snapshot "Discover Stories"

DISCOVER STORIES

My second coaching tip for those who know someone who needs to be reconciled to God is: *Take the time to listen and really understand their story.* Did you ever wonder why some really, really smart, wonderful people are not reconciled to God? Did you stop to think what their barrier might be? Have you ever asked them to tell you their story? And have you taken time to listen? This is part of what we need to do to help people connect with God.

I know a high-integrity, smart, compassionate business guy who might seem to an outside observer more "Christian" than many Christians. But by his own admission he wanted to stay at arm's distance from God. As our friendship grew, I worked up the courage to ask why he kept fending off God. I asked him to tell his story.

He said, "To be truthful, Bill, I wouldn't want to be a disappointment to God. I'm a man of my word. I keep my promises; I don't make commitments lightly. If I were to commit myself to God and promise to obey him and keep all the requirements of the Bible, I know right now I couldn't do it consistently. I'd fail. I would disappoint God. I don't want to be a disappointment to God."

Wow! What honesty. If I had not asked him to tell me what was standing in the way, and if I had not really listened to his story, I might have never known what kept him from drawing near to God. After he told me his roadblock to faith, I was able to open God's Word and show him that God calls us to receive and trust, not to be perfect. A few weeks later he called me long-distance and said, "I've received Christ and I am trusting that through His power I can live up to His standards." As I rejoiced with him, I was reminded in my heart how important it is to really listen to each person's story.

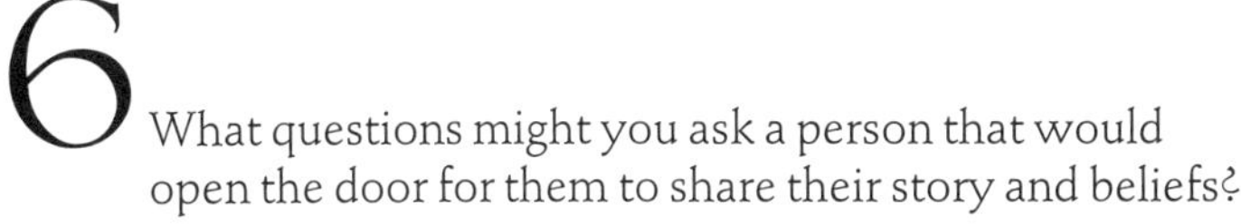

6 What questions might you ask a person that would open the door for them to share their story and beliefs?

How does a spiritual conversation change when we stop telling people what we think they should believe and begin asking them what they believe and why they believe it?

7 When you ask someone to tell you about their spiritual journey or life story, you will hear all sorts of things. How might you respond if a person told you they had *one* of the following barriers to faith:

- I think I have done too many bad things and God could never love me

- I've met too many people who claim to be Christians but seem to live messed-up lives with double standards
- I would like to come to God but I am waiting to clean myself up a bit and make my life more presentable to Him
- I have been hurt by the church or by Christians
- I don't think it is rational to believe in God

Read Snapshot "Pray for Open Doors"

PRAY FOR OPEN DOORS

My last word of counsel comes from Colossians 4:3. The apostle Paul talks about praying *for open doors*. This is so critical. When you have been an example of a reconciled life, listened to peoples' stories, and discovered their faith barriers, it is time to ask God to open a door so that you can tell the story of His grace and what He has done in your life. As you pray boldly for open doors, you will begin to see opportunities. When you do, test the door. Just push gently to see if it swings open. If you ask a few questions and the door seems open, walk through confidently. If the door seems closed, don't kick it in. Trust that God will give another opportunity, and keep praying.

Tell about a time you tested a door and it was firmly closed. How did you respond, and how did this experience impact the relationship?

Tell about a time you tested a door and it was unlocked and opened. What happened as you entered into that spiritual conversation?

PUTTING YOURSELF IN THE PICTURE

Test a Door

If you have known someone for a long time but have never really taken the time to give a gentle push on the conversational door, give it a try. Be prayerful, be humbly bold, and seek to enter into a spiritual conversation. You might be surprised that the door is more open than you think.

Hear a Story

Take time in the coming week to ask one person to tell you the story of their spiritual journey. Really listen. Seek to understand how they have arrived where they are. And remember, even an atheist is on a spiritual journey. It takes a lot of faith to believe that God does not exist!

Partners in Influence

Reflections from Session 5

1. If you have walked across a room or left your comfort zone to reach out to someone since your last group session, tell about your experience.
2. If you invited someone to tell you about their spiritual journey or life story since your last group gathering, tell about the conversation that followed.

THE BIG PICTURE

In ancient times most large cities were fortified with great walls. One way an army would capture a city was to lay siege to it. Not a single arrow was shot. There was no clashing of swords, no hurling of spears. Instead, they would surround a city and not permit anyone in or out, cut off the supply lines, and just wait. It was sinister ... and effective. When the food was gone or water ran out, the people trapped in the city would either surrender or die.

A story of a city under siege is found in 2 Kings 7:3–10. Enemy troops had surrounded Samaria and had been there so long that the people inside the city were starving. So terrible were conditions that four people with leprosy decided to sneak out and surrender to the army of Aram. They hoped perhaps that someone might show them some compassion. At the worst, they would be executed and die anyways.

As they approached the enemy camp, to their astonishment they discovered a ghost town—the entire army of Aram had fled. That very night God had caused the army of Aram to hear the sound of approaching chariots; in fear, they ran away, leaving all their provisions—food, clothes, silver, and gold. The men with leprosy were so excited! They ate and drank until they were filled. They gathered as much clothing and gold as they could carry and hid it where they could retrieve it later. Then they went back to the camp for another load.

Then something amazing happened. They began to think of all the people inside the walls who still believed an enemy army surrounded their city. They thought of all those who were starving and dying inside. And they concluded, "We're not doing right. This is a day of good news and we are keeping it to ourselves." What a moment of clarity! They went on to invite everyone in the city to come and share in the stockpile of food, drink, clothes, gold, and much more.

What a powerful picture for Christians and the church today. We have so many blessings, both physical and spiritual. How can we not run out into the world and invite people to share in this heavenly stockpile? How could we keep it all to ourselves? If we are not sharing Jesus with others, it might be time for us to hear the wake-up call and say, "We're not doing right. This is a day of good news and we are keeping it to ourselves."

A WIDE ANGLE VIEW

1 What blessings/good things do you have as a follower of Jesus that you would love to share with those who don't know Him? Answer this question by using *one* of the simple examples below:

- I long for (Name of person) to experience (Describe some aspect of God's character)
- I would rejoice if (Name of person) could receive (Tell about some blessing only God can give)
- I would be delighted if (Name of person) could be changed by the Holy Spirit (Tell about how God might transform this person)
- Anything else you want to share . . .

A BIBLICAL PORTRAIT

Read 1 Corinthians 3:5–9

2 The apostle Paul uses an agricultural picture to describe the work of evangelism. We have our part as God's

servants, but God has His part in the process of reaching people. What is our part in the evangelistic equation and what is God's part?

What does this passage say to those who take full responsibility for another person becoming a Christian and beat themselves up when people don't respond to the gospel?

What does it say to those who declare that it is all up to God and we don't have to do anything?

SHARPENING THE FOCUS

Read Snapshot "A New Definition of Success"

A NEW DEFINITION OF SUCCESS

We need a new definition of success when it comes to the reconciliation process. Too many Christians walk around feeling guilty that they have not pushed hard enough and pressed someone to become a follower of Christ. Too often we measure success only by identifying the very moment a person crosses the line of faith and accepts Jesus as Savior. I would suggest we see reconciliation as a process and learn to celebrate each step along the way.

Think about a scale going from –10 to +10. The –10 end of the scale is a person who is as far away from God as they can get. The +10 end is someone who is a fully developed and mature follower of Jesus. The 0 on the scale is the point of conversion.

Hostile to God	*Resistant*	*Curious*	*Accepts Jesus*	*Growing Believer*	*Fully Devoted*
–10	*–5*	*–2*	*0*	*+5*	*+10*

With this scale in mind, we can celebrate successes all along the continuum. If someone who is at –10 moves to –8 through connection and friendship with you, it is a success. If someone who is at –3 moves to –1 after you answer some of their spiritual questions, it is a success. They may not have crossed the line of faith, but they are closer. God has used you.

3 How might this definition of success encourage Christians and help us stay passionate about walking alongside spiritual seekers?

Read Snapshot "Partner with Other Believers"

PARTNER WITH OTHER BELIEVERS

Just like the apostle Paul wrote that he planted seeds, his friend Apollos watered them, but God caused growth, we are all in community as we seek to point people to Jesus. Paul knew he never did outreach alone. The work of reconciliation is always a team effort. We are just one link in a glorious chain of people who influence a life. Sometimes we get to be the final link as a person crosses the line of faith. Other times we are at the middle or the beginning of the chain. It is an honor to be anywhere in the process. And God gets the glory anyways.

We all have our own stories about how this works. Here is one of mine: Many years ago I befriended a very wild guy. It took me three years just to drag him out of the bars and interest him in reading the Bible. I prayed, tested the door, listened to his stories, and walked with this guy the whole time. Then he went on a sailing trip with a guy from Willow Creek. The first day of the trip, the guy just casually says to my friend, "Would you like to open up your life and receive Jesus Christ?"

My friend says, "I guess I would," and he prayed and received Christ right then and there. He called me on the phone and said, "Hey, Bill, John explained the message of Christianity to me. I opened my life up and became a Christian."

I said, "Put John on the phone!" I jokingly said, "Hey John . . . three years! You show up. One day. Unbelievable."

4 Tell about how God used a team of people, over time, to lead you to Himself and help you grow in faith.

5 How is God using you, in a team effort, to reach out to someone who has not yet received Christ?

How do you see your unique part in this outreach effort?

Read Snapshot "Partner with the Church"

PARTNER WITH THE CHURCH

We don't have to do the work of reconciliation all alone. God has given the local church to help us in our outreach efforts. From worship services to church dinners to youth events to holiday programs to small groups and much more, the local church is a great partner in this wonderful work of reconciliation. It does not matter if your local congregation has fifty people or five thousand, its warmth and love can always be an asset in our efforts to reach out with the grace of Jesus.

6 What are some ways your local church can serve as a partner as you reach out to people with the grace of Jesus?

What is one new ministry, program, or idea that might increase your congregation's outreach potential?

Read Snapshot "Partner with Christian Organizations"

PARTNER WITH CHRISTIAN ORGANIZATIONS

As we listen to people's stories, we may discover their barriers to faith sometimes need special partnership support. If you are walking with a person who is struggling with paralyzing addictions, you might want to connect them to a proven Christian recovery program. If they have suffered abuse as a child, invite a gifted Christian counselor to become a partner on your journey together. I once walked with a woman who had recently lost a child, and part of the process was her getting into a support group for people dealing with loss and grief. This partnership with a wonderful Christian group became part of her walk to Jesus. Even those dealing with financial stress can get a better understanding of God's presence and plan by attending a biblically based financial program. As you walk with people toward the Savior, don't walk alone; draw from the wealth of wisdom and strength of the many Christian organizations all around you.

7 What are some of the ministries and organizations you have partnered with through the years? How do they support those who are still investigating the Christian faith?

Read Snapshot "Partner with the Holy Spirit"

PARTNER WITH THE HOLY SPIRIT

Jesus was absolutely crystal clear on this topic. We can't do evangelism without the presence and power of the Holy Spirit alive in our lives. After he rose from the dead, Jesus said:

"But you will receive power when the Holy Spirit comes on you; and you will be my witnesses in Jerusalem, and in all Judea and Samaria, and to the ends of the earth." (Acts 1:8)

All through the book of Acts we see that direction and power for witnessing to the resurrection of Jesus came through the Holy Spirit. Just as the leaders of the early church needed the Spirit's power to bring the gospel, so we need His anointing and filling if we are going to be part of God's mission in this world and help reconcile people to God.

8 How do you see the Holy Spirit working as a partner in your call to be part of God's reconciling work in this world?

PUTTING YOURSELF IN THE PICTURE

Forging Partnerships

Take time in the coming week to pray in the following directions:

- Ask God to use you as a partner with other Christians to reach out to friends and loved ones. Also pray for God to bring many godly believers into the lives of people you are reaching out to.
- Pray for your local church to grow more and more committed to the ministry of reconciliation on every level. And

pray that you will engage in the opportunities afforded by your church.

- Make a list of local Christian organizations that exist to spread the gospel and support the local church. Pray for each of them, asking God's blessing on their ministry.
- Submit yourself to the leading of the Holy Spirit and pray that you will be responsive to any promptings and direction He seeks to give you.

Leader's Notes

Leading a Bible discussion—especially for the first time—can make you feel both nervous and excited. If you are nervous, realize that you are in good company. Many biblical leaders, such as Moses, Joshua, and the apostle Paul, felt nervous and inadequate to lead others (see, for example, 1 Cor. 2:3). Yet God's grace was sufficient for them, just as it will be for you.

Some excitement is also natural. Your leadership is a gift to the others in the group. Keep in mind, however, that other group members also share responsibility for the group. Your role is simply to stimulate discussion by asking questions and encouraging people to respond. The suggestions listed below can help you to be an effective leader.

Preparing to Lead

1. Ask God to help you understand and apply the passage to your own life. Unless that happens, you will not be prepared to lead others.
2. Carefully work through each question in the study guide. Meditate and reflect on the passage as you formulate your answers.
3. Familiarize yourself with the Leader's Notes for each session. These will help you understand the purpose of the session and will provide valuable information about the questions in the session. The Leader's Notes are not intended to be read to the group. These notes are primarily for your use as a group leader and for your preparation. However, when you find a section that relates well to your group, you may want to read a brief portion or encourage them to read this section at another time.
4. Pray for the various members of the group. Ask God to use these sessions to make you better disciples of Jesus Christ.
5. Before the first session, make sure each person has a study guide. Encourage them to prepare beforehand for each session.

Leading the Session

1. Begin the session on time. If people realize that the session begins on schedule, they will work harder to arrive on time.

2. At the beginning of your first time together, explain that these sessions are designed to be discussions, not lectures. Encourage everyone to participate, but realize some may be hesitant to speak during the first few sessions.
3. Don't be afraid of silence. People in the group may need time to think before responding.
4. Avoid answering your own questions. If necessary, rephrase a question until it is clearly understood. Even an eager group will quickly become passive and silent if they think the leader will do most of the talking.
5. Encourage more than one answer to each question. Ask, "What do the rest of you think?" or "Anyone else?" until several people have had a chance to respond.
6. Try to be affirming whenever possible. Let people know you appreciate their insights into the passage.
7. Never reject an answer. If it is clearly wrong, ask, "Which verse led you to that conclusion?" Or let the group handle the problem by asking them what they think about the question.
8. Avoid going off on tangents. If people wander off course, gently bring them back to the passage being considered.
9. Conclude your time together with conversational prayer. Ask God to help you apply those things that you learned in the session.
10. End on time. This will be easier if you control the pace of the discussion by not spending too much time on some questions or too little on others.

We encourage all small group leaders to use *Leading Life-Changing Small Groups* (Zondervan) by Bill Donahue and the Willow Creek Small Group Team while leading their group. Developed and used by Willow Creek Community Church, this guide is an excellent resource for training and equipping followers of Christ to effectively lead small groups. It includes valuable information on how to utilize fun and creative relationship-building exercises for your group; how to plan your meeting; how to share the leadership load by identifying, developing, and working with an "apprentice leader"; and how to find creative ways to do group prayer. In addition, the book includes material and tips on handling potential conflicts and difficult personalities, forming group covenants, inviting new members, improving listening skills, studying the Bible, and much more. Using *Leading Life-Changing Small Groups* will help you create a group that members love to be a part of.

Now let's discuss the different elements of this small group study guide and how to use them for the session portion of your group meeting.

The Big Picture

Each session will begin with a short story or overview of the lesson theme. This is called "The Big Picture" because it introduces the central theme of the session. You will need to read this section as a group or have group members read it on their own before discussion begins. Here are three ways you can approach this section of the small group session:

- As the group leader, read this section out loud for the whole group and then move into the questions in the next section, "A Wide Angle View." (You might read the first week, but then use the other two options below to encourage group involvement.)
- Ask a group member to volunteer to read this section for the group. This allows another group member to participate. It is best to ask someone in advance to give them time to read over the section before reading it to the group. It is also good to ask someone to volunteer, and not to assign this task. Some people do not feel comfortable reading in front of a group. After a group member has read this section out loud, move into the discussion questions.
- Allow time at the beginning of the session for each person to read this section silently. If you do this, be sure to allow enough time for everyone to finish reading so they can think about what they've read and be ready for meaningful discussion.

A Wide Angle View

This section includes one or more questions that move the group into a general discussion of the session topic. These questions are designed to help group members begin discussing the topic in an open and honest manner. Once the topic of the lesson has been established, move on to the Bible passage for the session.

A Biblical Portrait

This portion of the session includes a Scripture reading and one or more questions that help group members see how the theme of the session is rooted and based in biblical teaching. The Scripture reading can be handled just like "The Big Picture" section:

You can read it for the group, have a group member read it, or allow time for silent reading. Make sure everyone has a Bible or that you have Bibles available for those who need them. Once you have read the passage, ask the question(s) in this section so that group members can dig into the truth of the Bible.

Sharpening the Focus

The majority of the discussion questions for the session are in this section. These questions are practical and help group members apply biblical teaching to their daily lives.

Snapshots

The "Snapshots" in each session help prepare group members for discussion. These anecdotes give additional insight to the topic being discussed. Each "Snapshot" should be read at a designated point in the session. This is clearly marked in the session as well as in the Leader's Notes. Again, follow the same format as you do with "The Big Picture" section and the "Biblical Portrait" section: Either you read the anecdote, have a group member volunteer to read, or provide time for silent reading. However you approach this section, you will find these anecdotes very helpful in triggering lively dialogue and moving discussion in a meaningful direction.

Putting Yourself in the Picture

Here's where you roll up your sleeves and put the truth into action. This portion is very practical and action-oriented. At the end of each session there will be suggestions for one or two ways group members can put what they've just learned into practice. Review the action goals at the end of each session and challenge group members to work on one or more of them in the coming week.

You will find follow-up questions for the "Putting Yourself in the Picture" section at the beginning of the next week's session. Starting with the second week, there will be time set aside at the beginning of the session to look back and talk about how you have tried to apply God's Word in your life since your last time together.

Prayer

You will want to open and close your small group with a time of prayer. Occasionally, there will be specific direction within a session for how you can do this. Most of the time, however, you will need to decide the best place to stop and pray. You may want to pray or have a group member volunteer to begin the lesson with a prayer. Or you might want to read "The Big Picture" and discuss the "Wide Angle View" questions before opening in prayer. In some cases, it might be best to open in prayer after you have read the Bible passage. You need to decide where you feel an opening prayer best fits for your group.

When opening in prayer, think in terms of the session theme and pray for group members (including yourself) to be responsive to the truth of Scripture and the working of the Holy Spirit. If you have seekers in your group (people investigating Christianity but not yet believers), be sensitive to your expectations for group prayer. Seekers may not yet be ready to take part in group prayer.

Be sure to close your group with a time of prayer as well. One option is for you to pray for the entire group. Or you might allow time for group members to offer audible prayers that others can agree with in their hearts. Another approach would be to allow a time of silence for one-on-one prayers with God and then to close this time with a simple "Amen."

Daily Influence

1 Corinthians 13

Introduction

Christ-followers should never minimize our light-giving potential. Instead, we need to think seriously about ways we can make a difference by letting our light shine to chase back some of the darkness in our sphere of influence. Although we know the importance of bringing people to a state of reconciliation and relationship with God through Christ, it is also important that we exercise our influence in practical ways. In this session we will look at simple ways we can influence those around us through: having hearts filled with love, meeting practical needs, and confronting injustices in our community and world.

The Big Picture

Take time to read this introduction with the group. There are suggestions for how this can be done in the beginning of the leader's section.

A Wide Angle View

Question One Feeling that we can't make a difference or exercise influence is a serious problem. Almost every person who walks on this earth will deal with the enemy's insidious lies that make them feel they don't have much to offer. In dramatic contrast, Jesus wants us to know that we *can* let His light shine in our dark world. We *can* make a difference. We *can* all leverage our influence for His glory. If we allow our life to be put under a bowl, it will be diminished. But if we place it on a lampstand, the God of the universe can use our light to chase back some of the darkness that's in and around our sphere of influence.

A Biblical Portrait

Read 1 Corinthians 13

Question Two The apostle Paul, inspired by the Holy Spirit, pens an amazing list of love indicators — things that love is and things that love is not. Love is more than an emotional high; it is a choice to live a certain way. It is a daily commitment to be a certain kind of person by doing some things and avoiding other things.

As you walk through the passage, identify the "love is" and "love is not" items, being sure to look at each characteristic from both sides. In other words, if love is patient, it is fair to say that love is not *im*patient, pushy, or rushed. In a similar way, if love is not proud, it is fair to say that love is humble. Also, give real-life examples of what this love looks like in our relationships.

Question Three The apostle Paul begins this famous love passage with some qualifiers. It is important to recognize that this chapter of 1 Corinthians comes in a specific context. Chapter 12 is all about the use of spiritual gifts. Chapter 14 digs into how we need to demonstrate balance and wisdom as we use our gifts in community. At the start of chapter 13 Paul states that a person can speak in tongues, utter prophetic words, exercise great knowledge, have powerful faith, give with unbounded generosity, and even be martyred, but miss the wonder of God's gifts. Love must be the power that governs the use of all gifts. Without love, the gifts ring hallow; with love, the gifts make sense.

Sharpening the Focus

Read Snapshot "Spread Love" before Question 4

Question Four Much of what we do comes from what we see. All of us have a handful of people who have been models of godly, consistent love. As a group, celebrate these people by sharing stories of the example they have been in your lives.

Read Snapshot "Meet Needs" before Question 6

Question Six The old saying holds true, "Actions speak louder than words." When believers and a local church take action and meet needs, the message of Jesus is proclaimed, doors are opened, and the presence of God breaks into homes and cities. In the same way, when needs are right under our nose and followers of Jesus look the other way, we send a message that God does not care and that the church is impotent—and we miss amazing opportunities to spread the message of God's grace.

Read Snapshot "Confront Injustice" before Question 8

Question Eight Micah 6:8 says:

He has showed you, O man, what is good.
And what does the Lord require of you?

To act justly and to love mercy
and to walk humbly with your God.

We should all seek to use our influence for doing something beyond spreading love and meeting practical needs. When we see injustice in the world we should reflexively say, "That's not right; God can't be pleased with this." In such moments our heart should cry, "It's time that I step it up and use my influence to confront these wrongs!"

A number of years ago something took root in my life in regard to racial injustice. I've had lots of friendships across racial lines but in my heart I thought, "I'm not responsible; it's not my job to confront systemic racial injustices." But the more I learned about racial injustices, the more I felt the Holy Spirit tugging at my heart saying, "Bill, this is your issue . . . you have to do something." Since then I have been seeking to engage in God's work of overcoming racial injustices.

All of us can find our place in overcoming injustices. Some people might combat economic injustice by developing a microenterprise or supporting legislation that leads to fair trade. Others might build bridges between churches from various racial backgrounds. Some, convicted that hungry children should be fed and homeless people should have a bed to sleep in, will serve at a local soup kitchen or shelter. The opportunities for using our influence are nearly endless.

Putting Yourself in the Picture

Challenge group members to take time in the coming week to use part or all of this application section as an opportunity for continued growth.

DEEPER INFLUENCE

PSALM 140

INTRODUCTION

Daily influence grows as we spread love and meet needs. It also comes as we begin noticing and resisting injustices in the name of Jesus. But we can press even deeper with our influence. First, we can seek to stem the tide of violence in our communities and world. As we do this, we let the light of Jesus shine.

Beyond this, we are called to let the light of Jesus shine through our lives in a way that will help reconcile people to God. It is not enough to be nice, to love, to serve others. It is not even enough to battle injustice and resist violence. We are also called to enter into God's reconciling purposes in the world. We are to become agents of reconciliation as we bring the message of the cross, empty tomb, and the gospel to the world. The key is to live with a balance of meeting physical and spiritual needs. We are called to feed the hungry and offer the bread of life that lasts for eternity, Jesus.

THE BIG PICTURE

Take time to read this introduction with the group. There are suggestions for how this can be done in the beginning of the leader's section.

A WIDE ANGLE VIEW

Question One Even the strongest and most influential person can feel overwhelmed when we see the rising tide of sin, brokenness, evil, injustice, and violence in our world. But if each of us does our part, shines some light, and speaks out where God has placed us, God can change the world through His children.

A BIBLICAL PORTRAIT

Read Psalm 140

Question Two David is clear that there are evil people who do violence in this world. As it was then, so it is today. The problems are so prevalent that David cries out for protection over his own life. As we read David's words we discover that some people intentionally use their words and actions to do evil and violence. They set traps, look for victims, and take delight in their malevolent activities. At the same time, David is confident that God has His eye on the poor and broken. God sees, He cares, and He is ready to take action.

Sharpening the Focus

Read Snapshot "Stemming the Tide of Violence" before Question 4

Question Four There are a number of ways that believers today deal with the presence of sin, brokenness, violence, and pain in the world. Take time as a group to be honest about how we isolate ourselves from the realities all around us. Here are just a few thoughts to get the conversations started:

- *It's not my problem.* If the violence does not touch me or my family, I can ignore it.
- *They deserve it.* We can look at those who are bound in oppressive systems and tell ourselves that they must have done something wrong to earn such a fate.
- *There is nothing I can do.* We can feel overwhelmed and intimidated by the violence around us and avoid it, assuming our contribution would not make a difference.
- *I have my own problems.* We can so fixate and focus on our own problems that we have no energy to help others.

Read Snapshot "Reconciling People to God" before Question 6

Question Six Of course, many things mattered to Jesus, but when He gave His personal mission statement He was clear that the reason He left glory and entered human history was "to seek and to save what was lost" (Luke 19:10). In His own words Jesus was telling us that reconciling people to God was the main thing of His life and it should be atop our priority list as well. When we begin a new day we should pray, "Jesus, let me be an active part of Your reconciling work today." When we walk into a new situation we can quietly ask the Holy Spirit: "Give me eyes to see lost people as You do and a heart to care for them with the love of Jesus." When we put our head on the pillow at the end of the day we should dream about how God might use us in His redemptive and reconciling work the next day.

Read Snapshot "Striking a God-Honoring Balance" before Question 8

Question Eight If you read a description of the activities of the Acts 2 church, you discover that they were very balanced. This church did two things with enormous amounts of courage and intensity.

First, they fearlessly proclaimed the message of Christ. At the risk of their own blood, they went out and told people that they could be reconciled to God through Jesus, His Son. It is important to remember that those were the days when people were fed to lions for proclaiming the Christian faith! At the same time they battled the violent systems that led to poverty by selling their possessions and sharing them with those who had none. They did not just feel bad for the poor; they lifted them up and provided for their needs.

Putting Yourself in the Picture

Challenge group members to take time in the coming week to use part or all of this application section as an opportunity for continued growth.

Eternal Influence

Luke 15

Introduction

Jesus used three stories—the lost sheep, the lost coin, and the wayward son—to try to drive home to the Pharisees (and to us) something very profound. God's attitude toward all people, whatever their standing or circumstances, is that they really matter to Him. Indeed, lost people matter enough to God that He is willing to search them out and to give them opportunity for reconciliation through Christ. When any lost soul is retrieved, there is great rejoicing in heaven. This message encourages Christ-followers to not give up on anyone in their sphere of influence, but to go all-out in making sure all people know they matter to God.

The Big Picture

Take time to read this introduction with the group. There are suggestions for how this can be done in the beginning of the leader's section.

A Wide Angle View

Question One Have you ever lost a child, even for a few minutes? Have you lost a wedding ring, a pet, or something precious to you? If you have, you know the feeling in the pit of your stomach as you search, pray, and long to find that which is lost. As you remember this feeling of deep concern and longing, you get a little glimpse of how God feels about those who have not yet come to Him through faith in Jesus. God cares more than we can dream or imagine.

A Biblical Portrait

Read Luke 15

Question Two As we read Luke 15 we get a few lessons from the Master Influencer. Here's the background: Jesus was teaching in a public square and on this particular day a large group of nonreligious types had gathered around Him — secular people with all of their secular language, values, and lifestyle issues. This was the party crowd of Jesus' day, definitely not clean-cut, walk-the-line, upstanding folk. But the words and person of Jesus fascinated them.

While Jesus conversed with this secular crowd, an elite group of religious leaders looked on. These leaders, the Pharisees, began to mutter to one another about Jesus. It really bothered them that Jesus welcomed "sinners" and treated them with dignity. They became suspicious of Him because it almost appeared that He liked these people. Besides, they knew that Jesus not only welcomed these "sinners," but He had dinner with them. In the first century, when you ate dinner with someone, it was often a three- or four-hour affair. You spent the evening in their home and had many courses in a relaxed atmosphere. It was a very intimate occasion.

Jesus' behavior bothered the religious leaders for many different reasons. It violated their theology, their tradition, their social etiquette, their whole worldview. Rabbis were expected to keep their distance from such people.

Theologically, the Pharisees believed that God could barely restrain Himself from wiping secularized, sinful people off the face of the earth. They believed God was disgusted with them and was one provocation away from pelting down fire and brimstone upon them.

Jesus — the second person of the Holy Trinity, God Himself in the flesh — knew the truth about His Father's heart toward wayward, secular, nonreligious people. Jesus knew that the Pharisees' position was dead wrong.

So Jesus had a choice to make. Despite being in the middle of His conversation, He knew what the Pharisees were talking about. Was now the time and place to try to bring influence? Were the logistics right?

Jesus decided He would try to influence them. He didn't take a confrontational approach, but simply told three short stories. Nor did he take any time to explain them afterward. Master influencers often use creative approaches as well as time-delay influence techniques, sort of like time-release capsules of influence.

Jesus trusted that after He told these stories, later on some of the religious leaders would ponder His words and the light would go on. Maybe there would be some epiphany, a new understanding, and they would finally understand how God really feels about lost people.

Sharpening the Focus

Read Snapshot "Something of Value Is Missing" before Question 4

Question Four People ought to matter to us more than things. We don't use people to get things; we use things to serve people. People matter more than achievements or our reputations.

When we really come to grips with the fact that people are God's greatest treasure, and when others become a treasure to us, we get up in the morning and decide that today is going to be a day when we love people. Today we will serve people, feed someone who is hungry, clothe someone who is cold, embrace a new possibility, walk through an open door, and help someone be reconciled to God. Everything changes when we understand how precious people are to God.

Read Snapshot "Worth a Search" before Question 5

Question Five If we have a million dollars and drop a dollar, we might not even take the time to bend over and pick it up. If we have a pet, but we never really liked it, we might not bother to look for it if it runs off. But God is radically different than you and me. There is not a person on the face of this earth that He does not care about. With billions of people, He knows every name and cares for each one with infinite love. You were worth an all-out search, organized in heaven. And the people you care about who are still far from God are worth a search. As a matter of fact, that neighbor or colleague at work who bugs you on a regular basis, they are worth an all-out search too . . . just like you were.

Read Snapshot "Party Time" before Question 7

Question Seven There is something wonderful about entering into the heavenly party that happens every time a man, woman, or child comes to faith in God through Jesus. As individuals and as churches we should celebrate these amazing moments. It could be at a glorious outdoor baptism service, over a special dinner, or in a moment of a worship service when we stop and just celebrate God's goodness. We can be creative here, but it is important that we not miss these opportunities to throw a party, celebrate, and rejoice over God's goodness.

Read Snapshot "This Is Urgent" before Question 8

Question Eight There was a time in the history of Willow Creek when most of us carried around the names of three or four people who we were praying would open their hearts to the love of God. It was a common thing for us to stop each other and say, "Give me your card and I'll pray for whomever is on your list; you pray for mine." We had such a sense of urgency that prayer for lost people was on our hearts and lips on a daily basis.

Through the years I have known dozens of people who left promising careers in the marketplace to join church staffs (most at a significant pay decrease) because they wanted to give the best hours of their day to helping the local church reach its full redemptive potential. Their sense of urgency was so intense that they built their whole life around positioning themselves to share the message of God's love.

I could not recount the many, many times I have heard of believers who have strategically invited fellow believers and spiritual seekers to their home or out to dinner so that relationships could be bridged. These "Matthew parties" have led to more spiritual connections and fruit than I could possibly know. In all of these things and more, there has been a sense that we need to press forward because what we are doing matters. There is urgency to this call to let the light of Jesus shine in this dark world.

Putting Yourself in the Picture

Challenge group members to take time in the coming week to use part or all of this application section as an opportunity for continued growth.

THE ANATOMY OF SPIRITUAL INFLUENCE

2 CORINTHIANS 5:16–21

INTRODUCTION

Every Christ-follower is called to be an ambassador of reconciliation. This requires a serious commitment. Seeing people as Jesus sees them means looking past their flaws and desiring for them to be reconciled to God. Whether we personally initiate the process or whether we pray fervently that God will use others, we should long to see the hands and hearts of lost people be linked to the hands and heart of God.

We can use our influence in many ways. We can use it to be known around our workplace as a really nice person. We can use it to attain more money. We can even use it to try to end some kind of injustice. However, we must always remember that getting involved in God's reconciling work is by far the most important way to use our influence.

THE BIG PICTURE

Take time to read this introduction with the group. There are suggestions for how this can be done in the beginning of the leader's section.

A WIDE ANGLE VIEW

Question One When I got back to the marina I paid the young man who drove me to the camp and we said good-bye. He drove away and I returned to my boat, just vibrating with a sense of intensity. I felt so privileged that God would choose to use my influence to help a young man understand what it takes to be reconciled to God.

I get to do some pretty exciting things in my life. I race sailboats; I have a pilot's license and fly private planes; I travel to fascinating places. Amazing experiences, all. But none of it comes close to the thrill I feel when heaven and hell are at stake and a person is listening to the message that could change them forever. It's the highest-stake thing happening on planet Earth.

A Biblical Portrait

Read 2 Corinthians 5:16–21

Question Two Paul is talking about a restored and healed relationship with God the Father that comes as we understand the sacrifice Jesus made on the cross and the cleansing that comes because of His shed blood. If you want to dig deeper into this topic with your group, read Romans 5:9–11 and Colossians 1:21–23.

Sharpening the Focus

Read Snapshot "Influential Hands" before Question 4

Question Four In her late-high school and early-college years, my daughter Shauna wandered away from God. It was heartbreaking for my wife Lynne and for me. Try as we might as parents, we were clearly not the best ones to take her hand and reconnect it to the hand of God. Fortunately, God brought a wonderful group of godly college-aged women alongside Shauna and they became just what she needed. I am so thankful that God has His ministers of reconciliation all over the world just waiting to reach out to others. Since then Shauna has told some of her story in a book called *Cold Tangerines*. In it she describes these "sent ones" from God who looked past her sinful choices, past her drinking excess, past a lot of things not right with her life. They didn't try to shine her up; they just tried to hook her back up with God and get her reconciled to Him again.

Read Snapshot "Influential Eyes" before Question 6

Question Six In Mark 8 Jesus encountered a blind man who requested to be healed. Jesus took him outside the village, wet His hands and touched the man's eyes, and then asked him if he could see. The blind man said that technically he could see, but that the people looked like trees walking around (v. 24). It is like he was saying, "I can see, but I know I'm not seeing right."

Scripture says that Jesus touched his eyes one more time and restored his sight completely. That man needed a second touch so that his eyesight was perfectly clear. Maybe what we should begin praying is, "Lord, give my eyes another touch. Help me see people the way You do. Change my eyes!"

When I was in the car with that young man who drove me to the camp and back, I wasn't looking at his piercings, tattoos, or the holes in his jeans. I was looking at the hole in his heart. I was thinking about what could happen if that hole in his heart was filled up with the love of God. I had a picture of his hand in God's hand. That's what I was trying to see.

Read Snapshot "An Influential Heart" before Question 8

Question Eight It is time for God's people to dream, to be creative and try new things. Your group might want to do a variation on Matthew's party, hosting a small group party where each person invites one spiritually disconnected friend. Make it a time to hang out, make new friends, and build redemptive bridges. Or your group might want to take a mission trip together or serve a ministry in a neighborhood or city near your church. The key is, make your hands available, open your eyes to see, allow God to touch your heart, and then ... do something.

Putting Yourself in the Picture

Challenge group members to take time in the coming week to use part or all of this application section as an opportunity for continued growth.

NATURAL INFLUENCE

ACTS 16:16–34

INTRODUCTION

After reconciling us to Himself through Christ, God gave us the ministry of reconciliation. The question is, how do we initiate this ministry of reconciliation in a way that the non-believers with whom we have influence will want to reach out to God? This session focuses on three basic things that are important in the process of influencing people to reconciliation with God. First, we can live out a fully reconciled life as an example. Next, we can take time to listen as people tell their stories and seek to understand why they have not been reconciled to God. Then, we can commit to pray for open doors that will provide an opportunity to tell the story of God's grace and what He has done in our lives.

THE BIG PICTURE

Take time to read this introduction with the group. There are suggestions for how this can be done in the beginning of the leader's section.

A WIDE ANGLE VIEW

Question One I tell this story in greater detail in a book titled *Just Walk Across the Room: Simple Steps Pointing People to Faith.* This book, and the related church campaign, helps Christians and entire congregations learn to use their influence to bring God's love to the world in natural ways.

A BIBLICAL PORTRAIT

Read Acts 16

Question Two In Acts 16, Paul and Silas were arrested for spreading the message of Christ's love. After being stripped naked, beaten, and flogged, they were thrown into a dungeon to suffer and maybe die. In the darkness and filth of that cell,

Paul and Silas start singing to God, despite bleeding lips, aching pain, and open wounds on their backs. Amazing!

Then God caused an earth tremor strong enough to break open the cell doors, enabling Paul and Silas to escape. Though the hand of God freed them, their faithfulness had led to severe persecution and extreme physical abuse. What a reminder that following the will of God does not always lead us to a safe and secure place. No one was more faithful than Jesus, and He ended up on a Roman cross. As His followers we should always remember that Jesus called us to take up a cross and follow Him (Matt. 16:24).

Question Three The jailer on guard that night had fallen asleep. When he awakened and realized that all the prison cell doors were open, he was sure that Paul and Silas had fled. He immediately drew a sword to kill himself because he knew the authorities would kill him the next day for letting his prisoners escape.

Paul intervened. "Don't harm yourself!" he shouted. "We are all here!" Immediately the jailer asked, "What must I do to be saved?" This man had heard Paul and Silas sing through their pain; he now witnessed that they had stayed in their cells rather than escape. It was obvious to him that they were living out their faith.

What a great reminder that people are watching and listening all the time. Our example means more than we know.

Sharpening the Focus

Read Snapshot "Be an Example of Reconciliation" before Questions 4 & 5

Question Four Not everyone can set up a confession booth. But we can all be creative. Signs of God's kingdom and examples of God's reconciling presence in our lives come in many shapes and forms. From small acts of service to grand gestures of grace, we can all show the world that we have entered a new life through faith in Jesus. As a group, form a list of "light-shining" actions Christians can take as individuals, in small groups, and as a church. These can be things you are already doing, ideas you have heard from others ... or God might just inspire a creative new way to let His light shine.

Question Five Not only can followers of Jesus put their light on a stand, but we can also put it under a bowl. When we are petty, greedy, small-minded, insensitive, and do not exhibit the fruit of the Spirit (Gal. 5:22–23), we give the world a reason to wonder if our faith is real. The point is not that Christians have to live flawless lives ... that's impossible. But we should examine our attitudes and actions to ensure we are growing to look more and more like Jesus with the passing years.

Read Snapshot "Discover Stories" before Questions 6 & 7

Question Six When it comes to asking people questions about their own spiritual journey, it is important to do so with the right spirit. If we are just setting them up to tear them down, this will ring hollow. But if we are truly curious and care about the process that brought them to where they are, it will lead to a dynamic conversation. We might ask:

- Did you grow up going to church? If so, what was that like for you?
- Did your family celebrate any religious observances as you were growing up? If so, could you tell me about them?
- What is your understanding of God?
- Do you ever pray? If so, who do you pray to and do you get answers?
- I'd love to hear about your spiritual heritage.
- What keeps you from believing in God?

The issue is not so much the perfect question. It is being honestly interested in other people and hearing their story. As we listen, we will gain insight to what keeps them from God.

Question Seven This discussion is not about loading up with a specific presentation or memorized response when we identify a spiritual roadblock. It is about talking together and realizing that most of the reasons people stay away from God can be addressed with sensitivity and honest truth from God's Word and life. As others share and we listen, we can seek ways we might help them break down barriers that stand in the way of faith.

Read Snapshot "Pray for Open Doors" before Question 8

Question Eight Christians can make mistakes on both ends of the spectrum. On one end, we push too hard. The door is firmly locked and we start pounding or we get out the battering ram. This is not productive. When we hit a roadblock like this, it is time to step back, pray more, keep loving, and keep listening.

On the other end of the continuum, some of us won't even knock on the door or give it a gentle push to see if it swings open. If we tend to be the ultra-cautious type, we need to be bolder and test a few more doors. We might be surprised to discover that there are more open doors than we know. Jesus said, "The harvest is plentiful but the workers are few. Ask the Lord of the harvest, therefore, to send out workers into his harvest field" (Matt. 9:37–38).

Putting Yourself in the Picture

Challenge group members to take time in the coming week to use part or all of this application section as an opportunity for continued growth.

PARTNERS IN INFLUENCE

1 CORINTHIANS 3:5–9

INTRODUCTION

This session reminds us that it is not always the Holy Spirit's intention that just one Christ-follower is to be responsible for bringing a person who is far from God over the line of faith. Believers must be comfortable with taking only whatever steps, whatever conversations, seem relevant in their interactions—and then allowing the next believer or the next worship service to be a catalyst for continuing to move that seeker forward on the pathway to crossing the line of faith.

God uses individuals, churches, Christian organizations, and most of all the work of His Spirit to help people take steps forward in their faith journey. When we understand and embrace this holy partnership we can celebrate each step along the way and rejoice when a spiritual seeker moves a little closer to the heart of God.

THE BIG PICTURE

Take time to read this introduction with the group. There are suggestions for how this can be done in the beginning of the leader's section.

A WIDE ANGLE VIEW

Question One As followers of Christ, there are times when we drink fully of the blessings of God; moments when the sweet flavor of His grace overflows into our lives; when our prayers are answered, God's leading is clear, and we are aware of His guiding hand on our life. As God's people we are always aware that heaven awaits us and is our final destination. Add to this the fruit of the Spirit, fellowship with God's people, and every spiritual blessing in the heavenly realms and we should stand in awe of the stockpile of blessings we have as Christians.

In these moments, when we see a colleague, a neighbor, a friend, or a family member wandering far from God, our heart should ache. When we see a person missing the blessing of God and slowly self-destructing because of unwise decisions, our desire for them to know the Savior should grow large. We are like the four lepers who left the famine of the city to find a stockpile of more food, drink, clothes, and gold than they could ever use. Like them, we should run back to the city and tell everyone we see of blessings beyond description awaiting them if they will come to God in the name of Jesus.

A Biblical Portrait

Read 1 Corinthians 3:5–9

Question Two Paul is not trying to say that he and Apollos are worthless and added nothing to the outreach equation. To think this is to miss the whole point of this passage. Paul is using a hyperbole (an exaggeration used to make a point... we use them all the time!) to be clear that only God can draw a person and offer salvation. Were it not for the sacrifice of Jesus, the love of the Father, and the wooing of the Holy Spirit, no one would be able to come home to God. So, Paul did his part, Apollos did his, and God grows lives and saves! In the same way, we are an important part of God's redemptive work in the world, but only God can change a heart and He gets all the glory when someone repents of sin and comes to Him through faith in Jesus.

Sharpening the Focus

Read Snapshot "A New Definition of Success" before Question 3

Question Three For too long we have defined evangelistic success as the moment a person steps across the line of faith. Until our friend or family member actually calls out to Jesus, confesses their sin, and becomes a Christ-follower, we tend to feel like we have failed. But if we can see the process of reconciliation as a journey, we can celebrate each step forward. When someone goes from hard-hearted to open and interested, this is a huge change in the right direction. We can rejoice that things are moving forward and look forward to the next step.

Read Snapshot "Partner with Other Believers" before Question 4

Question Four It is not about us. It really isn't. We can scatter seed. We can water. Only God can grow a person and lead them to heaven. So let's drop all of the talk about what "I" have done and work together to point people toward Jesus. If we are there early in the redemptive process and don't get to see the final day of conversion, no worries! If we contribute in the middle of the process and are bringing influence in year five of a ten-year journey, praise God. We are part of the action and were able to see someone go from –8 to –5. If we are there when a person finally says yes to Jesus, this is a wonderful thing. But God gets the glory no matter where we come alongside in the process.

Read Snapshot "Partner with the Church" before Question 6

Question Six I have lost count of the number of times I have said, "The local church is the hope of the world." I believed that the first time I said it and I believe it even more today. If the church we attend is a biblically functioning community, it will be a great partner in our effort to shine the light of Jesus. The people who are part of our church can pray for and with us as we reach out. The warmth and welcome of the church should draw people in and reveal the presence of God. We ought to make every effort to support our church and trust that God will make it a partner in our evangelistic calling.

Read Snapshot "Partner with Christian Organizations" before Question 7

Question Seven Most Christian organizations have a heart to come alongside the local church in the work of evangelism. They are not an enemy to be resisted but a partner to be embraced. If we do happen to run across an organization that is down on the local church and feels a sense of competition, certainly we ought to use wisdom and be careful. But most Christian organizations have a love for the church and want to help us succeed in our ministry.

Read Snapshot "Partner with the Holy Spirit" before Question 8

Question Eight At the end of the day, the power and presence of the Holy Spirit in our lives is the key to evangelistic influence. Jesus was clear that we receive power when the Holy Spirit is at work within us. As we seek to be a person of influence in our circles, we need to ask the Holy Spirit to lead, move, and surprise us on a daily basis.

Putting Yourself in the Picture

Challenge group members to take time in the coming week to use part or all of this application section as an opportunity for continued growth.

Willow Creek Association

Vision, Training, Resources for Prevailing Churches

This resource was created to serve you and to help you build a local church that prevails. It is just one of many ministry tools published by the Willow Creek Association.

The Willow Creek Association (WCA) was created in 1992 to serve a rapidly growing number of churches from across the denominational spectrum that are committed to helping unchurched people become fully devoted followers of Christ. Membership in the WCA now numbers over 12,000 Member Churches worldwide from more than ninety denominations.

The Willow Creek Association links like-minded Christian leaders with each other and with strategic vision, training and resources in order to help them build prevailing churches designed to reach their redemptive potential.

For specific information about WCA conferences, resources, membership and other ministry services contact:

Willow Creek Association
P.O. Box 3188
Barrington, IL 60011-3188
Phone: 847.570.9812
Fax: 847.765.5046
www.willowcreek.com

Interactions Series

Big Questions

Clear Answers to Confusing Issues

Bill Hybels with Kevin and Sherry Harney

A PERSPECTIVE LIKE NO OTHER

Life is filled with big questions, and it seems everyone has a different answer. Whether from pop culture, political figures, conventional wisdom, or our friends, we are inundated with conflicting advice and opinions. Where can we go to find clear answers to the confusing issues we face?

God is ready to give us the wisdom and insight needed to navigate the questions that seem too big for us:

- Will wars ever cease?
- Can our planet survive?
- How do I balance life's demands?
- Is God really out there?
- Does God hear my prayers?
- Aren't all religions the same?

Answers to these questions are not simple. Only God has the vantage point needed to help us. He has a perspective like no other. God made the universe and holds it in His hands. He alone can answer our toughest questions.

Softcover: 978-0-310-28065-1

Pick up a copy at your favorite bookstore!

Interactions Series

Celebrating God

Discover the Truth of God's Character

Bill Hybels with Kevin and Sherry Harney

ARE YOU READY TO CELEBRATE?

A stadium full of football fans jump to their feet and cheer with deafening volume when a game-winning pass is caught. Family members gather every year to give gifts and sing choruses of Happy Birthday. Friends congregate just to have a party ... they hardly need a reason. In the Bible God instituted festivals and feasts. There is something in the human spirit that loves to rejoice, shout, and celebrate ... and God likes it that way.

We were created for celebration, and the focal point of our praise should always be God. When we get glimpses of His character, expressions of joy should spontaneously erupt. God is a refuge; He is generous and righteous, full of extravagant love toward us. The Maker of heaven and earth is relational, He guides us, and He will never leave us. It's time to discover God's character and make Him the focal point of our celebration.

Softcover: 978-0-310-28063-7

Pick up a copy at your favorite bookstore!

ReGroup™

Training Groups to Be Groups

Henry Cloud, Bill Donahue, and John Townsend

Whether you're a new or seasoned group leader, or whether your group is well-established or just getting started, the *ReGroup*™ small group DVD and participant's guide will lead you and your group together to a remarkable new closeness and effectiveness. Designed to foster healthy group interaction and facilitate maximum growth, this innovative approach equips both group leaders and members with essential skills and values for creating and sustaining truly life-changing small groups. Created by three group life experts, the two DVDs in this kit include:

- Four sixty-minute sessions on the foundations of small groups that include teaching by the authors, creative segments, and activities and discussion time
- Thirteen five-minute coaching segments on topics such as active listening, personal sharing, giving and receiving feedback, prayer, calling out the best in others, and more

A participant's guide is sold separately.

DVD: 978-0-310-27783-5
Participant's Guide: 978-0-310-27785-9

Pick up a copy at your favorite bookstore!